Irena Sendler
and the Children of the Warsaw Ghetto

by *Susan Goldman Rubin*

illustrated by *Bill Farnsworth*

Holiday House / New York

In memory of
Irena Sendler (1910–2008)
and to the children
she rescued
S. G. R.

To Susan
B. F.

Text copyright © 2011 by Susan Goldman Rubin
Illustrations copyright © 2011 by Bill Farnsworth
All Rights Reserved
HOLIDAY HOUSE is registered in the U.S. Patent and Trademark Office.
Printed and Bound in October 2010 at Kwong Fat Offset Co., Ltd.,
Dongguan City, Quang Dong Province, China.
The text typeface is Palatino.
The artwork was created with oil paints on canvas.
www.holidayhouse.com
First Edition
1 3 5 7 9 10 8 6 4 2

Library of Congress Cataloging-in-Publication Data
Rubin, Susan Goldman.
Irena Sendler and the children of the Warsaw Ghetto / by Susan Goldman Rubin ;
illustrated by Bill Farnsworth. — 1st ed.
p. cm.
ISBN 978-0-8234-2251-7 (hardcover)
1. Sendlerowa, Irena, 1910-2008—Juvenile literature.
2. Righteous Gentiles in the Holocaust—Poland—Biography—Juvenile literature.
3. World War, 1939-1945—Jews—Rescue—Poland—Juvenile literature.
4. Holocaust, Jewish (1939-1945)—Poland—Juvenile literature.
5. Jewish children in the Holocaust—Poland—Warsaw—Juvenile literature.
6. Jews—Poland—Warsaw—History—20th century—Juvenile literature.
7. World War, 1939-1945—Poland—Warsaw—Juvenile literature.
8. Warsaw (Poland)—Biography—Juvenile literature.
I. Farnsworth, Bill, ill. II. Title.
D804.66.S46R83 2011
940.53'18092—dc22
[B]
2010023667

I was taught by my father that when someone is drowning,
you don't ask if they can swim, you just jump in and help.
—Irena Sendler

Early in the morning of September 1, 1939, Irena Sendler and her mother huddled in their Warsaw apartment near the radio. The news was alarming. "We heard that German forces had crossed the Polish border at dawn," said Irena. In fact, World War II had begun.

During the first weeks of the war German planes bombed Warsaw, Poland, day after day, night after night. Buildings caught fire and burned. Terrified people scrambled for safety.

Irena Sendler, a young Catholic social worker, did her best to tend the wounded and bring bread to the needy. But more and more refugees, who had fled their towns or had been driven out, streamed into Warsaw as the Germans kept up their attack. By September 28, 1939, the Poles surrendered. On October 1 German troops entered Warsaw. The city and most of Poland fell under Nazi rule.

Irena immediately joined the resistance movement of the Polish Socialist Party. "At this point, along with my most trusted girl friends, I organized a special crew to save people that were most endangered," she said. Irena and her friends kept Jews from starving by issuing hundreds of false documents identifying them as Polish citizens. This entitled them to financial aid from the Department of Social Welfare in Warsaw.

Even though the Germans had forbidden anyone to help the Jews, Irena defied their orders. Aiding Jews was nothing new for her. Back in her student days at the University of Warsaw, Irena had protested when Jewish students were forced to sit separately on a "ghetto bench." "I always sat with the Jews," she said, "showing them my solidarity."

Now she worried about her Jewish friends in the Jewish quarter of Warsaw, known as the ghetto. It was already crowded, yet the Germans rounded up and packed thousands of Jews from the countryside into the ghetto.

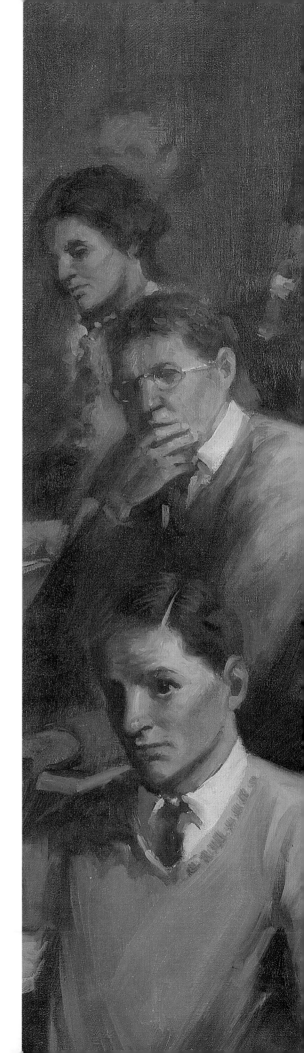

In May 1940 the Germans forced Jews to build a wall around the ghetto using bricks from bombed buildings. By November 1940 the wall was 11½ feet high, and topped with slivers of glass and barbed wire. Gates to the rest of Warsaw were guarded by armed police. Jews were forbidden to leave the ghetto, and the police shot anyone caught rescuing a Jew. The terrible overcrowding and poor sanitation caused a typhus epidemic. "The Germans were terrified of any epidemics," said Irena. "Therefore they allowed the Polish authorities to take care of the health and sanitation in the ghetto. Passes allowing us to enter the ghetto were given to us by the Warsaw Disease Control Department." Irena and her friends entered the ghetto dressed as nurses, in starched white uniforms and white caps. To show her sympathy, Irena put on an armband with the Star of David, just like the ones Jews were ordered to wear.

Inside, Irena was horrified by what she saw. "Old and young were dying on the streets," she said. Barefoot Jewish children in rags begged for bread or money and slept in doorways.

In July 1942 the Nazis started emptying out the ghetto. They herded Jewish children and adults into cattle cars going to Treblinka, a death camp, where Nazis would kill any Jews who had not already perished from sickness and starvation.

"The need to organize the removal of the children from the ghetto to the Aryan [non-Jewish] side became an absolute necessity," said Irena.

But how could she do it?

In December 1942 Irena joined the Council for Aid to Jews, a newly formed underground organization whose code name was Zegota. Irena met with the leader at a secret address. "He said that together we could do a great job because I had a network of trusted friends and he had money," she recalled. "Later he gave me the command of the Department of Help for Jewish Children."

Irena's code name was "Sister Jolanta." Barely 4 feet 11 inches tall, she risked her life when she disguised herself as a nurse and used a forged medical pass to enter the ghetto. Irena planned ingenious ways to smuggle out children. "Goodwill wasn't enough," said Michael Glowinski, one of the saved children. "The work had to be organized, methods of action well thought-out."

Irena's favored escape route went through the old courthouse, whose front faced the ghetto and whose back had an entrance on the Aryan side. "Some exits were open," said Irena, "and with the help of a brave custodian, it was possible to leave unnoticed." Nazi guards ordered children they suspected were Jewish to recite the Lord's Prayer. So before setting out, Irena taught the children how to make the sign of the cross and say basic Roman Catholic prayers.

Another scheme was to help teenagers escape with the "work brigade." The brigade consisted of skilled young people whom the Germans used in workshops on the Aryan side. Each morning the brigade left from an assembly point in the ghetto and returned at night minus those who had slipped away.

Many children fled through the sewers. These operations were timed to the second. "Me and my cousin, who was a little younger than me, stood in the gate of our house and were ready for our escape," remembered Piotr Zettinger, who was six years old at the time. "It was already dark, the street was deserted, and the silence was interrupted only by the echo of the marching soldier's boots." Somebody told Piotr to run to the hole in the middle of the road as soon as the soldier passed the gate and marched thirty steps farther.

"His steps were counted," said Piotr, "because suddenly I heard somebody whisper, 'Run!' and I felt a hand on my shoulder, maybe my mother's hand or my father's. They were bidding their good-byes forever."

Piotr and his cousin dashed to the middle of the street, where a manhole cover opened. "Another hand was waiting for me," said Piotr. "Somebody pulled me inside. 'Not a sound allowed,' said the stranger. 'You cannot talk or cough.'

"We walked behind this man, though we couldn't see him," said Piotr. "He carried a flashlight and lit it up from time to time."

Sometimes Irena hid children under the stretchers and floorboards in an ambulance. The trusted driver, Antony Dambrowski, kept a dog on the front seat. As the ambulance drove past the Nazi guards, Irena hit the dog's paw to make it bark and drown out any noises children made.

Other children were concealed in fire trucks. "The children had to be all covered in sacks, their heads invisible," said Irena. Usually she gave the younger ones a sleeping pill or taped their mouths so they wouldn't cry. She put some in body bags and coffins, and then she and a driver took them to the Jewish cemetery on the other side of the wall. If a guard stopped the truck, Irena claimed to be on her way to bury dead bodies.

Irena even dared to smuggle out babies tucked into potato sacks, suitcases, and toolboxes.

When Elzbieta Ficowska was six months old, her parents let Irena take her. Irena drugged Elzbieta and hid her in a carpenter's wooden box. The baby's parents slipped in a silver spoon engraved with Elzbieta's first name on one side and her birth date on the other. It is said that a carpenter carried the box right past the Nazi guards. According to another account of the rescue, Irena put the carpenter's box on a truck loaded with bricks, arranging the bricks so that air reached the infant. "It was a truly heroic act for my mother to give away her six-month-old baby with no guarantee it would survive," said Elzbieta many years later.

Persuading parents and grandparents to give up their children was often difficult. A mother might say yes, but then the father would say no.

"The one question every parent asked me was 'Can you guarantee they will live?'" recalled Irena. "We had to admit honestly that we could not, as we did not even know if we could succeed in leaving the ghetto that day. The only guarantee was that the children would most likely die if they stayed."

Once the children were out, Irena still had to hide them. She and her couriers moved the children from one safe house to another. Sometimes the first stop was Irena's apartment. Years later, men and women she had rescued remembered her holding their hands as they left the ghetto and even staying in her home.

"We had to try and teach the children to get used to the big change in their surroundings," she said. "They were now far from their dear ones. Often the only language they knew was Yiddish." The children had to learn to speak Polish and recite Polish songs, poems, and prayers so that "in any shelter on the Aryan side, they would look and sound like Polish children."

Piotr Zettinger, the boy who had escaped through the sewers, said, "I had to learn so much so quickly." Irena placed Piotr and most of the children in Roman Catholic convents and orphanages. Piotr wound up in a Catholic orphanage in Miedzles, Poland. "I knew I could count on the sisters," Irena said. "No one ever refused to take a child from me."

Irena placed some of the rescued children with Polish foster parents. "Private homes would agree to keep only very young children," she said. "Children in these loving homes suffered the least." Irena brought baby Elzbieta to a Polish Catholic midwife, who adopted the child and raised her as a Catholic.

Many times children had to be moved frequently because blackmailers threatened to turn children they suspected were Jewish over to the Gestapo for a cash reward. "This was tragic for the hidden child," said Irena. "Once I picked up a child that needed to go to another hiding place, and the child was crying endlessly. Through deep sobs he asked me, 'Can you tell me please how many mommies one can have? I am going to my mommy number thirty-two.'"

Irena gave the Jewish children Polish names and false birth and baptismal certificates. Haya Ester Shtein became Teresa Tucholska. Piotr Zettinger was allowed to keep his first name because it was a common Polish name, but he was not allowed to mention his last name or anything about his "ghetto mother or father."

"The Jewish children had to renounce their mothers and fathers in order to survive," said Irena. "They were taught day in and out, 'You're not Rachel, you're Roma. You're not Icek, you're Jacek.'"

Rachel, renamed Zosia, used to hide under her blanket at night and pretend to talk to her mother. "Why did you let me go?" she would whisper. "Why am I here? I want to be with you, Mommy. I am your little Rachel; I don't want to be Zosia."

It was difficult for Irena to keep any records at all. In April 1943 Jewish fighters organized an uprising in the ghetto, and the Germans retaliated by almost reducing the ghetto to rubble. Yet Irena and her volunteers continued getting people to safe havens.

Despite the chaos, Irena hoped to reunite the children with their families after the war. "We needed some way of remembering the children and their origins," she said. "We had to come up with some sort of list or card index." In "utmost secrecy" she wrote the children's Jewish names beside their Polish names "on a soft, transparent, narrow paper strip" and rolled it up. "I was the only one responsible for its safety," she said. At that time "anybody working with the underground had to be ready for an arrest at any given moment." Most people hid things beneath floorboards or in unused stoves, but Irena had another plan. "In case of a surprise search by the Germans," she thought, "I'll throw the little roll out the window and into a bush in the garden." She rehearsed many times in order to be "well prepared."

On the evening of October 20, 1943, Irena's aunt and Janina Grabowska, a dear friend and courier, came to visit. It was Irena's name day, and the women stayed up talking until around three o'clock in the morning.

Banging on the front door wakened them. It was the Gestapo, the German secret police! Irena immediately tried to throw the precious roll of names out the window, but the house was surrounded. Someone had informed the Gestapo of her underground activities. "The Germans were livid trying to enter," said Irena. "They were about to break the door. I threw the roll to my friend the courier and went to open the door." Eleven Gestapo burst in. "They lifted the floorboards and slashed the pillows," said Irena. "The horrific search lasted two hours. All this time I didn't even glance at [Janina] the courier so our frightened expressions wouldn't give anything away." The priceless roll of paper had to be protected. "Indeed, it was saved thanks to the courier's clear thinking and her bravery," said Irena. "She hid the roll in her underwear."

The Gestapo ordered Irena to get dressed. "I felt elated," she said, "and thankful that they didn't find the roll." She left the house still in her slippers and was escorted to a waiting car. She said, "The thought of what was going to happen to me struck terror in my heart."

The Gestapo took Irena to Pawiak Prison. There she saw several trusted friends, who had also been arrested. Irena realized that their secret meeting point, a laundry, had been discovered.

The Gestapo questioned Irena about the underground organization helping the Jews, its leader, and members. "They promised me that if I told them everything, I'd be released immediately," said Irena. "I was quiet as a mouse." For days they questioned and tortured her. During one brutal session the Gestapo broke Irena's feet and legs. She passed out. When she awoke, she still refused to talk. "After three months I was sentenced to death by a firing squad."

The Zegota leaders did not know that Irena's courier had hidden the roll of names. "The only thing I let them know in my letters," said Irena, "was that the Germans didn't find the roll. Zegota knew that the card index was their only chance to find the children after the war."

On the night Irena was to be executed, "the Gestapo truck driver, who drove a full truckload with us prisoners from the Pawiak to be shot, let me go," she said. The driver had received "a huge bribe delivered by a Pole who worked with the Germans." Irena's friends at Zegota had paid the bribe. At Na Rozdrozu Square the driver shouted, "Run!"

Irena hobbled away. A Gestapo document stated that she had been shot, and the Nazis believed she was dead. Two months later, even though Irena went into hiding, the Gestapo discovered that she was alive. "The Gestapo was after me again," she said. Irena sneaked her sick mother out of their Warsaw apartment, and they "moved [in] with strangers." Shortly afterward, Irena's mother died. Irena couldn't risk going to the funeral, because she knew the Gestapo would be there looking for her, and she was right.

For a while Irena stayed at a safe house where she had taken many Jewish children and adults: the Warsaw Zoo. During the early days of the war the zoo had been bombed and the zookeepers had freed some of the animals. The courageous Christian zookeepers had hidden Jews in the empty animal cages. Now Irena was one of their favorite "guests."

From her various hideouts, Irena continued working for Zegota. She had changed her appearance and had identification papers in a different name. Through the underground, she learned that the Polish Home Army was preparing to revolt against the Germans. A few days before the uprising began, Irena put the "miraculously saved list of children into two bottles and buried the list beneath an apple tree in the garden of another of her couriers, Jadwiga Piotrowska." Jadwiga lived right across the street from Nazi headquarters. Despite the risk, Jadwiga promised that if Irena died, she would take the roll of names "and deliver it to the right persons."

On August 1, 1944, the Warsaw Uprising broke out. Children, women, and Jewish volunteers fought alongside young Polish soldiers. Artillery shells crackled. Grenades exploded. The Germans bombed and torched building after building, killing everyone inside. The Polish soldiers hoped Soviet troops would arrive to help, but the Soviets never came. By October 2 the Germans had crushed the rebellion and Polish forces surrendered. Hundreds of thousands of people had died, and almost all of Warsaw had been destroyed. However, Irena survived. And her precious jars stayed safe and sound under the apple tree.

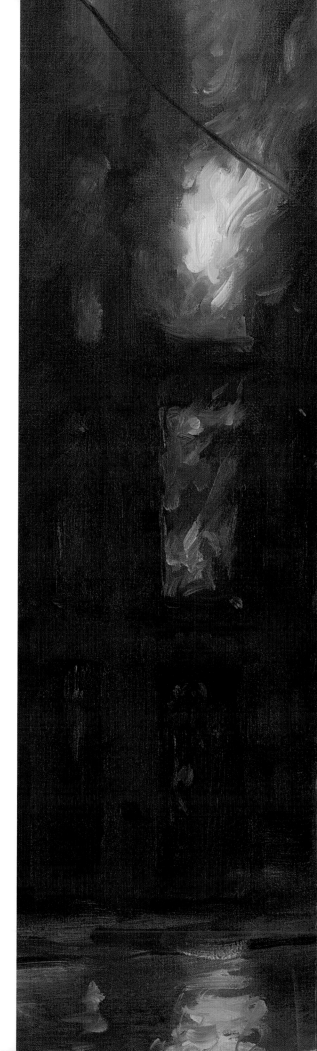

On January 17, 1945, Soviet troops finally liberated Warsaw. In the five and one-half years of German occupation, Irena had rescued nearly four hundred children; and under her leadership, Zegota had saved some two thousand children. The exact number is still uncertain. "After the war ended in Poland," said Irena, "I gave the card index with all the children's names to the head of the Jewish Committee, Dr. Adolph Berman." He was a member of Zegota. "With the help of the card index," said Irena, "the Jewish Committee placed the found children in orphanages or helped them to emigrate to Palestine" (which became Israel in 1948).

Many of the children grew up not knowing they were Jewish. Most of their parents and grandparents had been killed. However, the information on the card index allowed some children to rejoin their families. Piotr Zettinger's mother came to the monastery orphanage to get him. It had been three years since he had seen her, and he didn't recognize her. "The woman wore a dirty gray winter coat by far too big for her, her face was old, . . . and her hair unkempt and interwoven with gray strands," he said. But he left with her anyway, having become used to moving from place to place with strangers. They trudged along snowy roads to a station, where a locomotive steamed in. A man pulled Piotr onto the train. As it started moving, the woman who had been with Piotr was left behind. She frantically ran along the platform, waving her hands, shouting. The train slowed to a stop and the woman climbed up. "She pushed through, came close to me, hugged me, held me tight, and started to cry again," said Piotr. "This time I fully understood why. I met my mother."

Once when Irena was asked if she had rescued Jewish children for religious reasons, she said, "No, because my heart told me to."

Afterword

After the war Irena's story remained untold. The Soviets took over Poland and established a Communist government. The Communists regarded Irena as a traitor because she had worked with the underground, which had been supported by the anti-Communist Polish government-in-exile. Anti-Semitism swept through Poland again, and Irena was persecuted for having saved Jews. Quietly she resumed her career as a social worker in Warsaw and said nothing about her rescue operations.

But the children she had saved remembered her and talked about her. Teresa Tucholska Korner (formerly Haya Ester Shtein) said, "After the war Irena found me, and for the first few years I lived in her home until I finished secondary school." Irena helped Teresa rediscover her "Jewish roots," and later Teresa moved to Israel.

Piotr Zettinger went back to Warsaw with his mother and studied engineering at the university. "I saw Mrs. Sendler and paid a visit often," he said. "She lived quite near. As for many others, Irena Sendler was my good fairy."

Elzbieta Ficowska, the baby who had been smuggled out in a carpenter's box, grew up with her adoptive Polish mother, then married and had a family of her own. Irena was her daughter's "foster grandmother." Elzbieta said, "Mrs. Sendler saved not only us but also our children and grandchildren and the generations to come."

Irena's story finally emerged in 1989 when the Communist regime collapsed and Poland became a democratic republic. She received awards, honors, and worldwide attention. Yet Irena said, "It was always on my mind that I couldn't do more. This regret will follow me to my death."

When hailed as a hero, she said, "A hero is someone doing extraordinary things. What I did was not extraordinary. It was a normal thing to do.

"The real heroes were the Jewish children and their mothers, who gave away those most dear to their hearts to unknown persons."

Resources

Books

Ackerman, Diane. *The Zookeeper's Wife: A War Story*. New York: W. W. Norton & Company, 2007.

Adler, David A. *Child of the Warsaw Ghetto*. New York: Holiday House, 1995.

———. *A Hero and the Holocaust: The Story of Janusz Korczak and His Children*. New York: Holiday House, 2002.

Glowinski, Michael. *The Black Seasons*. Evanston, Ill.: Northwestern University Press, 2005.

Mieszkowska, Anna. *Mother of the Children of the Holocaust: The Story of Irena Sendler*. Translated by Kate Kingsford and Jedzej Buakiewicz. Warsaw: MUZA SA, 2007.

Scharf, Rafael, comp. Willy Georg, photographer. *In the Warsaw Ghetto Summer 1941*. New York: Aperture, 1993.

Weitzman, Mark, Daniel Landes, and Adaire Klein, eds. *Dignity and Defiance: The Confrontation of Life and Death in the Warsaw Ghetto*. Los Angeles: Simon Wiesenthal Center, 1993.

Articles

Attoun, Marti. "The Woman Who Loved Children." *Ladies' Home Journal*, December 2003.

Dolgin, Robyn. "Holocaust Heroine: Sendler's List Made a Difference." *Orange County Jewish Life*, July 2008.

Dunin-Wasowicz, Krzysztof. "Warsaw Polish Uprising." *The Encyclopedia of the Holocaust*, vol. 4. New York: Macmillan Publishing Company, 1990.

Gessner, Peter K. "Irena Sendler: WWII Rescuer and Hero." Info Poland, University of Buffalo, State University of New York.

Gutman, Israel, ed. "Warsaw: Jews During the Holocaust." *The Encyclopedia of the Holocaust*, vol. 4. New York: Macmillan Publishing Company, 1990.

———. "Warsaw Ghetto Uprising." *The Encyclopedia of the Holocaust*, vol. 4. New York: Macmillan Publishing Company, 1990.

Hevesi, Dennis. "Irena Sendler, Lifeline to Young Jews, Is Dead at 98." *New York Times*, May 13, 2008.

Jones, Maggie. "Irena." *New York Times Magazine*, December 28, 2008.

Levine, Samantha. "A Saintly Smuggler." *U.S. News & World Report*, October 27, 2003.

Snyder, Donald. "Irena Sendler's Legacy." *Magazine. The Jerusalem Post*, November 9, 2008.

Woo, Elaine. "Irena Sendler, 1910–2008, WWII Savior of Young Jews." *Los Angeles Times*, May 13, 2008.

Videos

Courageous Heart of Irena Sendler. Jeff Most/Jeff Rice Productions and Hallmark Hall of Fame Productions, Inc. April 19, 2009.

Life in a Jar: The Irena Sendler Project. Funded by the Milken Family Foundation and the Lowell Milken Education Center, 4 South Main, Fort Scott, KS 66701.

Testimonies from Yad Vashem Reference and Information Services

A nine-page testimony of Irena Sendlerowa given to Yad Vashem by the ZIH (Jewish Historical Institute) in Warsaw, 1966. Its number in the archives is Record Group O.33/file 6222. Translated from Polish to English by Anna Gelbart.

A one-page statement of Irena Sendler to the ZIH about her contacts with Jews in Warsaw during the occupation. Translated from Polish to English by Anna Gelbart.

The 1965 testimony of Teresa Tucholska Korner, nee Haya Ester Shtein, born 1929. Record Group O.3/file 2824. Translated from Polish to English by Anna Gelbart.

Stories Unpublished in English

"Meeting On A Train" by Piotr Zettinger, translated from Polish to English by Anna Gelbart.

"On the Common Path" by Piotr Zettinger, translated from Polish to English by Anna Gelbart.

Interviews with the Author

Piotr Zettinger, telephone conversations, August 5, 2009; September 16, 2009.

Correspondence

Tomasz Prot, deputy chairman, Association of "Children of the Holocaust" in Poland, e-mail messages to author, Friday, July 17, 2009.

Piotr Zettinger, e-mail messages to author, Saturday, July 25, 2009; Wednesday, July 29, 2009; and Tuesday, August 4, 2009.

Source Notes

Page 3: "I was taught . . . in and help." Irena Sendler, quoted in Levine, "A Saintly Smuggler."

Page 3: "We heard . . . at dawn." Irena Sendler, quoted in Mieszkowska, *Mother of the Children of the Holocaust*, p. 4.

Page 4: "At this point . . . most endangered." Irena Sendler, ZIH Testimony given to Yad Vashem.

Page 4: "ghetto bench." Irena Sendler quoted in Mieszkowska, p. 3.

Page 4: "I always sat . . . my solidarity." Ibid, p. 3.

Page 6: "The Germans were . . . Disease Control Department." Irena Sendler, ZIH Testimony.

Page 6: "Old and young . . . on the streets." Ibid.

Page 6: "The need to . . . absolute necessity." Ibid.

Page 9: "He said that together . . . Help for Jewish Children." Irena Sendler, quoted in Mieszkowska, p. 11.

Page 9: "Sister Jolanta." Ibid., p. 9.

Page 9: "Goodwill . . . well thought-out." Michael Glowinski, quoted in Ibid., p. 21.

Page 10: "Some exits were . . . leave unnoticed." Irena Sendler, quoted in ZIH Testimony, point 3.

Page 10: "work brigade." Ibid, point 6.

Page 12: "Me and my cousin . . . our escape." Piotr Zettinger, "On the Common Path."

Page 12: "It was already dark . . . soldier's boots." Ibid.

Page 12: "His steps were . . . good-byes forever." Ibid.

Page 12: "Another hand . . . time to time." Ibid.

Page 15: "The children had to . . . heads invisible." Irena Sendler, ZIH Testimony.

Page 17: "It was truly . . . would survive." Elzbieta Ficowska, quoted in "Irena Sendler's Legacy" by Donald Snyder.

Page 17: "The one question . . . if they stayed." Irena Sendler, quoted in Woo, "Irena Sendler, 1910–2008."

Page 18: "We had to . . . like Polish children." Irena Sendler, ZIH Testimony.

Page 18: "I had to . . . so quickly." Piotr Zettinger in e-mail message to author, August 4, 2009.

Page 18: "I knew I could . . . child from me." Irena Sendler, quoted in www.auschwitz.dk/Sendler.htm, page 2 of 5.

Page 21: "Private homes . . . suffered the least." Irena Sendler, ZIH Testimony.

Page 21: "This was . . . hidden child." Ibid.

Page 21: "Once I . . . number thirty-two.'" Ibid.

Page 22: "ghetto mother or father." Piotr Zettinger in e-mail message to author, Auguest 4, 2009.

Page 22: "The Jewish children . . . you're Jacek." Irena Sendler, ZIH Testimony.

Page 22: "Why did you . . . want to be Zosia." Ibid.

Page 25: "We needed . . . or card index." Ibid.

Page 25: "utmost secrecy." Ibid.

Page 25: "on a soft . . . paper strip." Ibid.

Page 25: "I was . . . its safety." Ibid.

Page 25: "anybody working . . . given moment." Ibid.

Page 25: "In case of . . . in the garden." Ibid.

Page 25: "well prepared." Ibid.

Page 26: "The Germans were . . . open the door." Ibid.

Page 26: "They lifted . . . in her underwear." Ibid.

Page 26: "I felt elated . . . find the roll." Ibid.

Page 26: "The thought of . . . in my heart." Irena Sendler, quoted in Mieszkowska, p. 13.

Page 29: "They promised . . . released immediately." Ibid., p. 15.

Page 29: "I was quiet as a mouse." Irena Sendler, quoted in Attoun, "The Woman Who Loved Children," p. 100.

Page 29: "After three . . . firing squad." Irena Sendler, quoted in Mieszkowska, p. 15.

Page 29: "The only thing . . . after the war." Irena Sendler, ZIH Testimony.

Page 29: "the Gestapo truck . . . let me go." Ibid.

Page 29: "a huge bribe . . . the Germans." Ibid.

Page 29: "Run!" Mieszkowska, p. 16, and "Sendler's Children," *The Polish Voice*, September 25, 2003.

Page 29: "The Gestapo was . . . again." Irena Sendler, ZIH Testimony.

Page 29: "moved [in] with strangers." Ibid.

Page 31: "guests." Ackerman, *The Zookeeper's Wife*, p. 166–167.

Page 31: "miraculously saved . . . Jadwiga Piotrowska." Mieszkowska, p. 16.

Page 31: "and deliver it . . . right persons." Irena Sendler, ZIH Testimony.

Page 35: "After the war . . . to Palestine." Ibid.

Page 35: "The woman wore . . . gray strands." Piotr Zettinger, "Meeting On A Train."

Page 35: "She pushed through . . . my mother." Ibid.

Page 35: "No, because . . . told me to." Irena Sendler, quoted in Mieszkowska, p. 18.

Page 37: "After the war . . . secondary school." Teresa Korner, quoted in Mieszkowska, p. 20.

Page 37: "Jewish roots." From Maria Thau, "Comments on the subject of the testimony given by Mrs. Teresa Ester Stein-Korner," Yad Vashem Reference and Information Services, translated from Polish to English by Anna Gelbart.

Page 37: "I saw . . . quite near." Piotr Zettinger to author, August 4, 2009.

Page 37: "As for . . . my good fairy." Piotr Zettinger, quoted in Mieszkowska, p. 22.

Page 37: "foster grandmother." Elzbieta Ficowska, quoted in Mieszkowska, p. 23.

Page 37: "Mrs. Sendler saved . . . generations to come." Elzbieta Ficowska, quoted in Hevesi, "Irena Sendler, Lifeline to Young Jews, Is Dead at 98."

Page 37: "It was always . . . do more." Irena Sendler, quoted in Levine, "A Saintly Smuggler."

Page 37: "This regret . . . to my death." Irena Sendler, quoted in Dolgin, "Holocaust Heroine."

Page 37: "A hero is . . . normal thing to do." Irena Sendler, quoted in Attoun, p. 104.

Page 37: "The real heroes . . . unknown persons." Irena Sendler, quoted in Mieszkowska, p. 19.

Acknowledgments

I thank my editor, Mary Cash, for responding to Irena Sendler's story the minute she heard it and taking it on as a project. At Holiday House I also thank John Briggs, Terry Borzumato-Greenberg, Barbara Walsh, Claire Counihan, and Pam Glauber for their ongoing support. I am deeply grateful to Adaire Klein, director of Library & Archival Services at the Simon Wiesenthal Center Library, and to Fama Mor, volunteer archivist, for helping me find primary source materials at Yad Vashem in Jerusalem, Israel, and at the Association of "Children of the Holocaust" in Warsaw, Poland. My warmest gratitude to Tomasz Prot, deputy chairperson of "Children of the Holocaust," for putting me in touch with Michael Glowinski and Piotr Zettinger, two of the children saved by Irena Sendler.

I particularly want to thank Piotr for talking with me over the phone and generously sending me his stories "Meeting On A Train" and "On the Common Path." Special thanks to Anna Gelbart for skillfully translating these stories and the testimonies of Irena Sendler and Teresa Korner from Polish to English.

Acknowledgments would be incomplete without mentioning George Nicholson and his assistant, Erica Silverman. And of course, a huge thank-you to Lunch Bunch for their helpful critiques and unflagging interest.

Index